Budget Scrapbooking
for Beginners

By Phyllis Matthews

Copyright 2012

DISCLAIMER

ISBN-13: 978-1481056731

ISBN-10: 1481056735

Table of Contents

INTRODUCTION: THE COST OF SCRAPBOOKING

A venture into the world of scrapbooking usually begins with a trip to the hobby store. There you peruse the aisles overwhelmed by the spectacular array of lovely textured papers in every color in the known universe. You relish down row after row of delightful stickers and embellishments, and you eye shiny new tools that cause your crafter's soul to drool with desire. But, those papers cost an average of a dollar for a single sheet. Only a dollar, you think without surmising the expense totaling up twenty or thirty times over for an average scrapbook.

The embellishments are five dollars or more per package, and I will never forget paying that amount for a single miniature Christmas tree laden with sparkling garland and ornaments. It was truly a work of art, but I will never succumb to that temptation again. On careful examination after removing it from the packaging, I easily learned how I could have produced the item myself.

The latest scrapbooking gadgets average from fifteen dollars to hundreds of dollars for a stencil cutting machine. The commercials for these appliances can easily induce you into a scrapbooking frenzy of desire. Keep the desire, but save your dollars. Most of the fancy tools I have purchased lie unused in cabinets and drawers.

Store advertising tactics convince you that you will need all the latest stickers, embellishments, acid-free adhesives, ribbons, sheet protectors, and an expensive album in which to place it all. When it all comes down to the facts of the matter, it is all made of paper, plastic, and textiles.

Why not use creativity instead? Your scrapbooks will not only cost far less, they will be uniquely yours. Through the years you will treasure the books even more that contain little bits and pieces of found objects from your own closets, cabinets—or trash bins. Who says the creative mind can't be practical?

Admittedly, whimsy does tend to like a free rein. The unfettered nature of the imaginative spirit does not like to be hampered by pragmatic matters—such as finances. However, if you must live on a budget, remind yourself that you will be able to make even more scrapbooks if you can find a way to do it for less. This book will show you how to save money and still produce some of your most artfully produced books ever.

You will need pictures, of course—the main ingredient. They will need to be printed, and at three to seven per page, this is one expense which is unavoidable whether you have them professionally produced or use your own computer and printer. The cost of the ink and paper usually is equal to most of the discount offers that are out there. Watch for specials in the photo department at your local discount stores, and shop online for good deals, too.

Acid-free adhesives—ranging from double-sided tape, glue sticks, dimensional dots, and liquid glues—amount to as much as three or four packages per scrapbook. One roll of acid-free double-sided tape is almost six dollars. This is why it is not unusual to spend over a hundred dollars to produce a single masterpiece. Until I learned some tricks of my own, I could hardly keep the cost under that amount. There are many creative ways to create budget scrapbooks that look anything but cheap and you can even have more fun making them. Read on!

CHAPTER 1. DOLLAR STORE FINDINGS

Most dollar stores have a scrapbooking section, and their papers are offered at about half the price of hobby stores. Typically, you can get a package of four to six sheets for a dollar. They are sometimes not as thick—which doesn't matter at all. And, I have found them to be exceptionally beautiful, with sparkles, glitter, and various dimensional effects. The packages are usually themed, so you can easily find something that coordinates well with your subject matter—whether it is vacations, sports, springtime, holidays or birthdays. There you will also find stickers and other adornments, although there are usually fewer to a package than those from the craft stores. How often do you end up with half-used packages of stickers anyway?

Their simple basic albums sell for only $5.00 as apposed to $20.00 or even up to $50.00 in the expensive stores. They may not be made as quite as well, but I have found them sturdy enough. They tend to be simple and in ordinary basic solid colors. As for them being plain—that's an easy fix. I have added ribbons, stickers, and even flowers to my album covers. I once cut through the front cover with a sharp X-Acto knife to make a window, and I often re-cover the whole thing with vinyl, cloth, or special paper to match the theme of the scrapbook.

The one I did for my "moving to the country" memory book is completely wrapped in burlap with a tiny scarecrow doll attached. The new baby scrapbook I made for my daughter-in-law was one of these bargain albums which I adorned with row after row of pink velvet and silk ribbons. For another similar book I printed my twin granddaughters' newborn pictures onto cloth which I adhered to an otherwise simple album, covering it completely. I used a simple iron-on printer sheet for the photo, and then I sewed that to pink cloth using a fancy stitch on my sewing machine, completely refurbishing a bargain-priced album. I added pink and green decorative braid from the sewing department as well. The possibilities using these techniques are endless.

Hair adornments also make dainty, frilly scrapbook embellishments, and you will find an enormous variety in any dollar store. Not only do they have bows small enough for scrapbooking purposes, but ribbons and bands can be found in a smorgasbord of colors and styles to fit your theme. After you remove the clasps, staples, or wires, they no longer resemble their original purpose at all. Cut through an elastic headband and it becomes a piece of ribbon or braid. Tape the two loose ends to the back of the page.

The advantages to paper sticker bands and borders from the scrapbooking store are many: 1) the colors and designs are offered in enormous variety, 2) the cloth adds texture which contrasts well against all the paper items on the page, and 3) it is easy to sew buttons or charms onto cloth hair adornments that are too plain for your needs. I did this on a Christmas page using a simple red headband by attaching it horizontally then sewing on silver teddy bear charms that dangled along the bottom edge.

Junk jewelry, a notorious dollar store find, can work as excellent embellishments as long as they are not too thick. Look for flat pieces or charms that are reasonably thin. Pendants are good. I use tiny beads all the time to drape across a page loosely or to border a picture frame. Look in the closeout section for good bargains on bracelets, necklaces, earrings, and decorative pins. Don't be afraid to tear something apart, and don't worry if you only need one part of a particular piece. It's cheap enough, and you can save the rest for another project.

Shop in the seasonal merchandise area in the dollar stores—and especially check into the out-of-season section to get those really rock-bottom prices. There is a better selection, though, if you splurge and get to the current stuff as soon as it hits the shelves. Just try to remember to keep your objects fairly flat. I found glittery snowflakes originally meant to be tree ornaments and some adorable gift tags with really cute graphics. All I had to do was cover the "to" and "from" wording with a sticker, some glitter, or a jewel. Christmas colored ribbons and bows are as great on a page as on a package. Halloween is another time to find a good selection of thrifty decorations, as is Easter. Halloween and Easter greeting cards are not so commonly sent out and so do not sell like Christmas cards. So you can always find such cards on sale immediately following the holidays. Their graphics are perfect for scrapbooks. I like to cut them up and use them like stickers—even the sentiments work great as text on your pages.

Joy was a cupcake with a cherry on top. Junior a cowboy complete with guns.

The title graphic for this page was a greeting card; underneath the card is black felt; the dangling border was a headband which I snipped the elastic off; the background is ordinary construction paper; I printed the text on colored copy paper.

The variety of commercially available greeting cards will give you astounding choices in every subject area. And, in the dollar store the price is right. Sometimes you can get them at two or three for a dollar. That certainly beats the price at regular stores where they are often four or five dollars each. At that rate, you can buy two or three of each and make them three dimensional by cutting out figures and gluing them over the original image for a special raised effect. Glue down the background first, then cut out a feature on another copy of the same card and attach it with a pop-out material over the same graphic you already pasted down. And, don't pay for the fancy pop dots. Use a piece of cotton of some foam insulation tape. The final result looks the same, and it's really crazy to spend money for things that don't even show.

In the stationery section you will not only find the greeting cards, but party goods and wrapping paper to use in many creative ways. Gift wrap can be cut up into 12 x 12 pages, and as long as you mat your photos with acid-free paper, it will work just fine. If it is too thin, back it with some cardboard. The piece that comes inserted inside the page protectors would be fine. It's already the correct size. You could even use this kind of paper to cover the outside of an album, but you will need to coat it well with contact cement or a similar adhesive. Otherwise, you are headed for puckers that will eventually tear.

In the party goods area, don't forget to check out the tissue paper, streamers, and tablecloths. Even the cake decorations offer lots of possibilities. Tissue paper can be used in much the same way as vellum on a page, only it's more delicate, so you need to work with care. Oh, and tissue paper is acid-free, so you can use it behind pictures for a really nice effect. Layers of multicolored tissue petals make beautiful and nicely flat flowers for your pages.

Use the actual tablecloth from the party, cutting it up into 12 x 12 size or smaller to use on your pages—the parts that don't have cake and ice cream dripping from them. This way your backgrounds can actually match the pictures from the party—and everyone will wonder how you did it. The goody bags look cute on the page, and you can stick something inside them.

Sometimes you can even use the cake decorations on pages, if they are made out of plastic rather than sugar. The little graduation caps from the cupcakes at my granddaughter's party worked great as charms on the page. I just snipped off the plastic picks with my scissors.

I cut Curious George from a leftover paper plate to make a graphic for my grandson's party page. Trim graphics from the party napkins then modge-podge (half white glue/half water) them to your scrapbook page. Since the napkin is so thin, the effect is like a printed picture on the page. This is a very delicate operation. Brush the medium on gently or the napkin will bunch up or tear.

The toy aisles should never be overlooked. Kids like stickers, too. And, although they may not be acid-free, that is okay as long as you don't put them directly onto photos. The offerings in this section are especially great for kid pages. You can find TV characters to match your child's favorites or to accompany a themed birthday party page. I have also used rub-ons, removable tattoos, and card games to add the kid factor to a scrapbook and make it truly unique. You can make your own three-dimensional charms with air-dry molding compound for kids. Use rubber stamps to make your impressions or use the little plastic molds that usually are included with the kids' play set for clay activities.

I once made a mini-album out of a child's vinyl purse. I kept it so that it opened on top like a real purse, and I left the straps on so that my granddaughter could carry it around. All I really needed to do was slit open the sides and attach the pages inside. I had to custom fit the shape of the pages to fit the purse, but that was worth the effort. I used paper from a sketch pad because it was sturdy and had a nice texture. You could do the same thing with a CD wallet, and the advantage is that the plastic sleeves are already inside.

Try using a small flat coin purse with either a snap closing or a zipper to make a little pouch on a page to hide a secret note or special treasure. Glue it with a strong adhesive. This would be a great way to display tickets to an event— just leave them sticking out through the opening.

CHAPTER 2. SEWING NOTIONS

You can buy scrapbooking embellishments that look like lace, buttons, ribbons, braid, and rick-rack. Or, you can use actual lace, buttons, ribbons, braid, and rick-rack. Most people would agree that the real thing looks even better. The dimensional effects are very attractive enhancements to your pages. Sewing and scrapbooking work well together, and much of the skills for both are the same—cutting, measuring, joining, and designing.

That expression "cute as a button" came from somewhere you know. Buttons—actual, real buttons—are sold at scrapbooking stores. They cost triple what they cost in the sewing department of a typical discount store. And, they aren't any better.

Use buttons to attach pictures to pages. Sew them on with wire, dental floss, or fishing line. Or use a dab of glue. If you glue them, you will want to thread them anyway for a realistic effect. I like to combine buttons with other materials to make flowers, too. A button makes a perfect center for a daisy. It makes cute wheels for trains, planes, or automobiles. I once glued three progressively larger white buttons to a dark blue page to make a really adorable snowman. I covered the holes with white glue and snowy glitter. Attach tiny blue or brown buttons to a paper doll for eyes that really catch your attention. You need really large faces or really small buttons for this to work. If the eyes are too big, it can look downright freaky.

Use binding tape, braid, or rick-rack to make borders, stripes, or edgings just as you would paper ones. They come in a variety of colors and patterns, so you can easily choose ones that coordinate with your pages. I once did a page about the dresses I made for my granddaughters, and I used some of the leftover rick rack as a border. If you can't find color you want, just buy white—then paint it, dye it, or use markers or crayons to make it anything you want.

Lace works well in a variety of methods. You can actually cover an entire page with a 12 x 12 piece of lace fabric as a background effect. It makes a beautiful wedding display, but if colored paper shows through it can apply to a prom theme as well as with pink for a baby girl. Lace works well for any feminine, dainty, or girly subject. I once spray a piece of lace with gold paint and placed it over black paper to make a Victorian mood in a book about my ancestry. You can even use lace as a stencil. Put the lace over your background paper, paint over the whole thing, then remove the lace when it is almost dry. It will make a reverse print of the lace on your paper. The trick is in the exact right degree of dryness—too wet and your design will smudge, too dry and it might stick, probably tearing your paper.

Even though you can't actually feel the difference through a plastic page protector, you can definitely appreciate the look of real textiles as opposed to the flat look of graphic fakes. I do like to incorporate some sensory effects whenever possible. Rather than see a pretty bow smashed behind plastic, I like to punch a little hole through the protector sheet right over the ribbons so that I can pull it through to the outside. This gives you the best of both worlds—preservation for your pages along with the ability to feel the beautiful textiles. You can do this with all kinds of objects just by slitting the plastic.

Grandma didn't get to go on the
Disney Cruise, but the dresses she
made for Hannah and Eden did.

The background for this page is an actual scrap of the material I used for the dresses. The banner across the top is a strip of organza ribbon attached with buttons.

Use eyelets from the sewing aisle as another method to attach pictures and other embellishments to your pages. Just punch the holes, insert they eyelet, and then hammer it down the same way you would with a piece of cloth. You can do this to your photos, too—with or without matting. Then run narrow ribbon or cord through the holes to the back side of the page, taping it there where it won't show. It also looks cute to weave ribbon through the

18

eyelets in a way that connects the pictures together in a loose scallop across the page.

Appliques and iron-ons make great decorations, too. But be careful. They can be pricey. Check the bargain bins, or better yet—tear them off unwanted pieces of clothing before you toss them out. Baby and children's clothing offer a gold mine of adorable features to place in your scrapbooks. I love to find lovely embroidered appliques so that people will think I spent hours doing the handiwork myself.

If you failed at Quilting 101, you may have another chance with a scrapbook page. No stitching involved, and the size is way less intimidating. No need to cut hundreds of tiny pieces of cloth—only enough to cover a 12 x 12 space—at most. You simply glue the design together instead of making all those intricate, tiny hand stitches. Simulate the stitches by making dashes with a felt tip pen. This may be time consuming, but if you want to highlight granny's quilting skills, a booth at the local fair, or decorate a country-themed page, this is a great way to do it.

Tulle—that's the stuff you buy by the yard to make tu tu's. It looks like netting, and there are limitless numbers of ways to use it in a scrapbook. The fact that you can see through it lends it to all kinds of possibilities. Put a strip down the side of a page, attach lettering and borders to make a gorgeous title or headline. Sew a tube, fill it with confetti, then flatten it for your page. Make a pouch or envelope with it and place a special little card inside, like an invitation or a note with a cute message. I used a gathered piece of white tulle to make a tiny baptismal gown on a page. Tiny pearl beads and thin ribbons tied the bodice and arm pieces to create the correct shape and add novelty. The same method could be used to make a wedding veil or a prom dress. Combine tulle with silk, brocade, or lace.

Velvet adds much beauty and femininity to a scrapbook. You can emboss velvet with your rubber stamps and a hot iron. Lay the velvet right side facing your rubber stamp against imprint side, dampen the back side with a cloth, and iron at a high temperature on the back side of the velvet for a minute or two. The imprint of the letter or graphic from the rubber stamp imprints into the material with a shiny permanent mark. Use simple shapes for the best results. A single letter, as for a monogram, works better with this technique.

Felt can be used any way that you would normally use paper. Attach embellishments to it; cut it into shapes; layer it; sew it, or write on it with glue or markers. If you do want to make a mat for a photo out of felt, use brads, buttons, or eyelets to attach the picture. Or, cut slits to attach it at the four corners by tucking the photo through the slits.

You can create art with zippers. The shiny metallic teeth add interest and give your page an edgy look. Cut the zipper in half by snipping off the bottom end. Trim some of the cloth away so that you have mostly metal with a tiny band of color with which to work. It's flexible enough to curve into spirals, swirls, or curves. Or, attach your photos to the cloth portion leaving the metal part to act as a border around the edge. I have already glued a zipper pocket on my page to hold miniature charms. Glue carefully so that the zipper will still open and close easily.

Yarn is an extremely versatile medium. You can weave it, braid it, wrap it, or sew with it. It comes in a myriad of colors and textures. Some even sparkles with glittery highlights. Some are feathery and light, while others are course like twine. You can string beads on it, sew it onto paper with a large needle, or make it into tassels for a graduation cap or a tail for a pony—either on a horse or the head of a paper doll. I once sewed brightly colored yarn to highlight our trip route onto a road map in a vacation scrapbook.

Sewing on paper with yarn or embroidery thread opens a whole new spectrum of scrapbooking possibilities. Try using a sewing machine and an ordinary spool of thread. I often sew pictures directly onto pages or onto the matting. If you do this, do not run your needle through any part of the page that contains glue. Use tape to hold it while you are sewing; just be careful not to get it near the stitching. Not only will your sewing machine needle become a gummy mess, but the paper will not feed correctly under the presser foot causing the stitches to space unevenly and inevitably tangle your bobbin. Even if you are not a sewer, I'm sure you can tell just from the description that this is a very undesirable situation. Try this first with some scrap pieces of paper, and if it doesn't go smoothly, settle for sewing your page by hand with a large needle and thread.

CHAPTER 3. KITCHEN AND HOUSEHOLD ITEMS

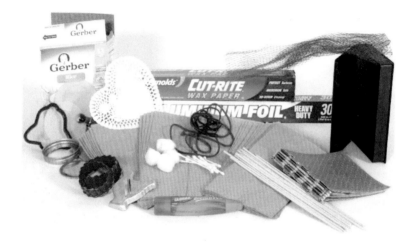

Trace cookie cutters to make paper, felt, or foam shapes for every holiday and season you can imagine.   Santa's, shamrocks, and Easter bunnies are the obvious choices, but simple shapes like stars and bells should not be overlooked.   If you have a set of concentric circle cookie cutters, you are set and have no need for an expensive circle cutter. I spent ten dollars for one of those and never could get it to work right. Cutting by hand takes a lot more time, but part of the fun of scrapbooking is using scissors and paper. It's almost as therapeutic returning to the nostalgia of kindergarten. You not only save the expense of fancy machines—you can skip those sessions with your therapist as well.

If I can't find a round cookie cutter the right size for my purpose, I look for a tin can or a drinking glass to trace. Yes, unless you have the unswerving hand of a surgeon your circles will have occasional little jags and bumps along the edge. As my grandmother used to say, "If it were perfect, it would look store-bought instead of hand-made." Who wants that? Your work will have more meaning and more sentiment attached with every little imperfection.

Food packaging—cereal boxes, produce netting, foil or plastic lids, foam trays, and cellophane windows are all completely free scrapbooking materials. Why pay for cardboard to build a pull-out infrastructure or sliding mechanism when it isn't going to show anyway? I built a little sliding car that glided along a cardboard slot on my page all from a cereal box. Sometimes, you aren't able to find card stock in the exact color you want. Paint your cardboard packaging material or cover it with paper or cloth of your choice, and you will never know its humble beginnings.

Foam meat trays, thoroughly cleaned of course, are easy to cut into shapes to adorn pages. They are, after all, the same Styrofoam you pay money for in the craft store. You can use the pointed end of a skewer like a stylus to impress these with designs or even make a custom stamp for inking or painting. This material can become any kind of feature or creature that you can imagine.

Cellophane windows from bakery goods can become windows for beads, stickers, charms, or ribbons to suit the theme. I cut a piece of cellophane into a sunburst shape and used dimensional glue around the edges to create a thin pocket to hold a spoonful of sparkling beads. When completely sealed, I had a shaker embellishment that really added a fun aspect to the cover of a vacation scrapbook. I did a similar trick using a round shape to make baby rattles on a book celebrating the births of my grandchildren.

Mason jar lid inserts make excellent small round frames for photos. I made some to represent Christmas tree ornaments by adding sparkle and paint. I used one to make a miniature metal pan for a pizza I cut from a magazine ad. I removed a wedge to show more of the metal pan. This worked really well on the page celebrating our pizza party.

Paper doilies were invented to place under the party foods on buffet tables. Over the years they have been used in pre-school craft projects and all kinds of creative endeavors. They now come in all kinds of shapes besides the traditional round ones—hearts, ovals, and rectangles. These have endless applications. They come in many colors, but I like the white ones which can be painted to coordinate with any kind of page perfectly. Large ones can become the background for an entire layout, and smaller ones can be used as matting for photos or grouped across a page to make an eye-catching display. Used just like lace, you can make a reverse imprint on paper for a cool effect.

Cupcake baking papers are cute, especially the multicolored ones. Since the inside is flat and the outside is pleated, they make excellent frames for round photos. This shape lends itself well to creating paper flowers as well. Try cutting the edges with decorative scissors for an unlimited variety of uses. Folded them into wedges, and try some origami techniques. Try dipping the edges in glitter to add some sparkle.

I love aluminum foil. It looks like metal, which is great for more masculine subjects or for an ultra-modern, trendy look. The heavy duty weight can actually be embossed by gently rubbing with a pencil eraser over rubber stamps. Do this carefully so that you don't tear the foil. If you make words, remember to spell them backward so the impression side will read correctly. Medium weight foil can be used to cover a cardboard shape, or it can be crumpled and re-opened to make an eye-catching background sheet.

The title for this page is embossed aluminum foil; the border is yarn; the little "to do" messages are printed on colored copy paper then cut apart with decorative scissors.

Wax paper is a great tool because stuff doesn't stick to it. Use your printer to print out your lettering on plain paper, cover it with wax paper, then outline your words with puffy paint or glitter glue. This does not work for smaller

27

more intricate fonts. Use larger block letters or a widely spaced cursive style of lettering. When dry, you can peel off the letters and glue them to your page. If it seems like it might break, just trim around the wax paper instead with fine point scissors.

Here's another tip for using wax paper. Fold a length in half. Open it up, sprinkle crayon shavings generously over one half then close the top half over it. Place a heavy grocery bag under and over your crayon shavings enveloped with wax paper. Then, iron gently at low heat, checking frequently under the paper bag to see if it's melting correctly. You don't want the wax paper to burn or turn brown. When it seems to be melted completely, remove the bags and allow the envelope to cool thoroughly. It will harden enough so that you can cut shapes like hearts, circles, or stars—but not anything too detailed. These make thin embellishments to glue or dangle from your pages. It is advisable to seal the edges first, just to make sure that the crayons won't re-melt if your book is exposed to heat. Seal the edges with white glue or acrylic sealer then dip it in glitter or cover the edge with some sparkly trim or ribbon.

Q-tips make great applicators for glue, paint, chalk, or ink. You can't beat the price as compared to the tools in the craft stores. In fact, I did an entire graphic once by dipping and pressing, dot by dot, onto a blank sheet of art paper. The result was like pointillism—maybe not museum quality—but it was pretty good for a humble scrapbook. I wouldn't attempt an intricate work of art, but a butterfly or a tree full of apples is easy enough for anyone to do.

Cotton balls make fluffy rabbits, cute snowmen, and lots of precious white creatures. They also work well underneath your paper objects to create a raised, three-dimensional effect. Craft stores actually sell foam dots for this purpose—and they are up to five dollars for a package. Just glue a cotton ball to your page, then glue your embellishment to the cotton.

Dental floss is both stronger and cheaper than thread for attaching buttons or charms to pages. I really like the red and green kind for Christmas pages. I hardly use the clear kind. But, once I made a tiny fishing pole with a twig, and it looked just like fishing line.

A bleach pen—normally used to remove stains from your laundry—is a great way to write on colored paper. The words or design you draw will beach out to a pale shade within a few minutes. Make big words or shapes. It doesn't work as well for fine details because it runs a little. Sometimes, that is exactly the effect you want. I made a simple "Yay!" on a dark maroon paper for a cheer-leading page. People wondered how I did that. Or make freehand swirls, loops, waves, zig-zags, etc. Use the pen to coat the surface of a favorite rubber stamp and make subtle faded impressions all over a page to create a wallpaper effect. Make simple stripes using a ruler.

An aluminum soda can provides excellent metal for a scrapbook page. It cuts so easily with simple scissors. Open it flat and use the back side to stencil on your shapes, and then cut them out. Just be careful. It is very sharp, but the danger is worth the risk of a little shed blood. You can paint it or keep the metallic colored graphics on the can. It almost tempts you to choose your beverages according to their colors.

Shaving cream mixed half and half with white glue makes very snowy-looking puffy paint. Cut out your shapes from cardboard because regular paper will get too soaked. Let it dry thoroughly then glue your shapes and letters to your pages. Titles on winter themes look great topped with dripping snow.

Skewers can be used to make scrapbooks. They are called piano hinge books, although I can't say I know why. It probably refers to the metal hinges which continue down the entire length of a piano lid. Use 11 x 17 paper, available at some discount stores, but always in stock at an office supply store. Fold each sheet in half, making four pages 11 x 8-1/2. Make as many as you want, but you will need an odd number. Stack them on top of each other, and cut ten 3/8" deep horizontal slits along the folded 11" side of each of the folded the edges. They will be about one inch apart, so you will need a total of ten slits making 11 one-inch wide tabs. These slits you will cut into "v" shaped cuts. Then you weave bamboo skewers—that's right, the same thing you use to make kabobs—through the slot of one folded page then the slot of the adjacent folded page, all the way through to the end alternating from the first to the second page. Repeat the process with the second and third pages, then the third and fourth pages. This is easy, but it may require a picture to make the method clear enough to understand. (See the following illustrations.)

These are the pages cut to size, folded in half, and with the snips cut into the folded sides.

Weave the skewer through the top channel then the channel of the next page. Just weave back and forth. When completely woven, snip off the skewers near the edge of the pages.

Paper lunch bag scrapbooks have become popular, and I think this had its beginnings in pre-school classrooms. The fold at the bottom of the bag makes for a unique peek-a-boo feature in the book. Remember to alternate your bags so that the bag bottom ends up on both sides of your book equally. Use an odd number of bags, fold them in half, punch holes equal distance from the top and bottom, then tie them together with ribbon or yarn. Cut your papers to the dimensions of your open pages, and make smaller cuts of paper for inside the pockets and openings created by the bag bottom and openings at the top of the bags. This give you lots of cute places to hide surprises. (See Illustrations.)

580 | 9781481056731 | 580

Location:　B1

VOM.H3

Title:	Budget Scrapbooking For Beginners
Cond:	Good
User:	vo_list
Station:	DESKTOP-95EUL5F
Date:	2020-03-17 18:46:54 (UTC)
Account:	Veteran-Outsource
Orig Loc:	B1
mSKU:	VOM.H3
Seq#:	580
QuickPick	SWS
unit_id:	191947
width:	0.26 in

delist unit# 191947

XXXXX

Glue the wrong side of the paper underneath the flap of the bag bottom; then fold it around the bag bottom, gluing as you proceed. Glue the paper down to the opposite side. Continue gluing papers end-to-end covering the open ends as you go.

Be sure to alternate colors and patterns. As long as your papers are cut to the dimensions of the paper bag, you will end up with fold wrapping around the open ends of the bag.

One pointer you might want to keep in mind: folding the finished bags in half and stacking them directly on top of each other will cause your top and bottom pages to recede gradually. You may not like that effect. I prefer to fold each bag in half, then stack the folded bags. Just punch your holes about a quarter inch from the fold and an equal distance from the top and bottom. Punch your holes *after* you adhere your scrapbooking papers. You can still use yarn or ribbon to tie the book together. I like the idea of using a grommet on the holes to prevent tearing. You can also use the larger grocery bags as well to make a larger book.

CHAPTER 4. KID CRAFT MATERIALS

One really good way to save money on making scrapbooks is to use the white inserts inside the plastic sheet protectors instead of fancy papers. This can make for a very creative outlet for the kid inside you. Use crayons, water colors, markers, chalk, etc. to decorate your pages with your own original artwork. Don't think you need to be an artist to do this. A swirl, a blotch, a few lines can take on a creative essence once it appears on a page. Most of the page is covered with photos anyway. Just think in terms of getting some color on the page.

Here are a few idea starters:

1) Write a message faintly in pencil, trace over it with white crayon, then dabble water color paint over the whole thing. You can sop up excess drips with a paper towel. The messier it turns out, the more artistic it will look.

2) Write a faint swirl, spiral or wavy line in faint pencil. Then use a sharpie pen to write your message in your own handwriting following the pencil line. Erase the line afterward.

3) Make streaks with colored chalk. Then use a sharply pointed chalk eraser to remove sections revealing the white background.

This page was done with simple markers and stamping.
The background was made with smudges of chalk.

This is the beginning...
February 3rd,
2005

It may take me a year to finish this book. In fact it might take five years. It's not that I think my thoughts are so important that they need to be recorded for posterity—or that I love creating—putting down words on paper and embellishing them with colors and themes. That's part of it. But most of all, I am thinking of some possible future great-great-great grandchild of mine who would love to know about my life and the times in which I live.

This page uses simple stamping as a background, and then pencil lines were made to guide my handwriting.

Use coloring book pictures as patterns for paper applique treatments. If done correctly, you will not even be able to tell the image came from a child's coloring book. Shop for generic pictures rather than popular characters so that you will get more use from them. Holiday books will provide many really cute pictures to use for your scrapbook pages as well as other crafting projects. Paper dolls can be used in the same way, and you can make your own clothes for them to match the people in the photos. Scan your pictures first so that you can have a guide as to how the pieces fit together after you've cut them apart to stencil onto colored construction paper.

Picture books, especially old ones, make really quaint decorations for your pages. If you don't want to cut out the illustrations, scan them. That's often a better idea anyway, so that you can use them multiple times. Look for pictures that go well with the theme of your scrapbook. A child's dictionary typically holds lots of pictures of objects. Try to find books with animals, babies, flowers, and scenes from daily life. I love the really old "Little Golden Books."

For this page I painted a water color border, and printed the picture on vellum then tore the edges.

Use children's molding dough that can be dried to a hard pottery-like material to make custom charms and embellishments. Some are air dried, others use a low temperature oven. Roll some out very thin and cut shapes to impress with words, names, or rubber stamp images. Make tiny holes and adorn them with ribbons. Press jewels into the clay to make tiny crowns or necklaces.

I used this kind of material to make miniature french fries which I painted golden and dabbled with red nail polish for ketchup. This was very impressive in a McDonald's box which I cut down to make smaller and thinner on my page. We had visited a McDonald's on vacation which is famous for its large play-land. Such an experience deserved to have a double spread in my vacation scrapbook, and no one can resist touching the french fries because they look so real.

Pipe cleaners have long been swiped from the toy box for a multitude of adult uses. They come in many colors and can be formed into loops, waves, and spirals. Since they are basically fuzzy wire, you can use them for the same functions—attach dangling things, make hinges for tiny booklets, or form them into letters.

Foam letters and shapes for children work just as well on your page as the ones from the hobby store, only they are cheaper. You can also find blank sheets to make your own creations. This medium offers many advantages: you can sew on them, punch holes in them, glue them, or layer them together. They can be painted, written on with pen or marker, and they cut easily. You can smudge them on the edges with ink or chalk. The combinations of all these techniques make for an endless variety of adaptations.

Use small sheets to cut out frames, text boxes, or large ones for title tags for your pages.

Game pieces, if they are small and flat enough are cute and colorful on a page. One of my favorites is scrabble tiles. I am always looking for them at yard sales. Once a few letters become lost, the game doesn't play right anymore. The property cards from a Monopoly game would be great on a page about a new home purchase—especially if you can find street names that match. Consider yourself lucky if you live in an area where the streets are named after states. Domino pieces are a little too thick to use, but an impression could be made of them using vellum paper, metal, or foil.

Playing cards, especially the Kings, Queens, Jacks, and Aces make colorful and interesting embellishments on a page about a game night at a casino—or a vacation in Las Vegas. They could represent a gamble of any kind, as could a few poker chips. A glued on "full house" could be a metaphor for a family growing larger, or a set of aces could be used to emphasize a test or exam someone passed with flying colors.

Glitter glue is an amazing invention. It's like paint, only it shimmers, and you can sprinkle tiny beads, sand, or jewels into it because it is sticky enough to hold objects. And, it dries hard. Squirt a spiral shape onto a piece of cardstock, press a round matted photo into the middle, and you have an eye-catching display for a really special subject. This glue is usually not acid-free, so don't let it actually touch your pictures. Use matting.

Tiny children's puzzles—the cheapest ones—makes great scrapbooking material. They are great as mats for individual letters to spell out titles. First, paint the puzzle pieces in colors to coordinate with your page, then glue on letter stickers or draw them on by hand with a sharpie pen. You can actually create a puzzle from a photograph by gluing it to a puzzle you don't want. Print the picture on very thin paper so you can press the edges into the creases while the glue is wet. This method is sometimes not as successful with photos of people because it's difficult to not get the separations over parts of the face. Scenic shots look great as puzzles. Want a really interesting look? Remove one piece of the puzzle deliberately, making sure it isn't from an essential part of the picture. This would be a good way to re-cycle those puzzles that have missing pieces.

This is an album cover which I cut through and made a window to place tiny beads. The title was made with painted puzzle pieces. The lettering is made with a sharpie.

Use Popsicle sticks in lots of cute applications. Make a photo into a Popsicle or a lollipop. Cut out your pictures into the correct shape, glue a Popsicle stick on the back and your subject has been turned into a sugary treat. For extra realism, take a little snippet of cellophane, scrunch it together in the middle with string or ribbon, then tuck the top half under the picture so that the bottom half rests over the stick. For an over-the-top treatment, make a lollipop from a picture of a child eating a lollipop.

You can write on Popsicle sticks with a Sharpie to add names, messages, etc. You can build them into frames for pictures or text boxes by tying the corners with string, wire, or ribbon. Glue a whole bunch together into a flat rectangle to use as a mat for a picture or text box. Make a fence out of them to decorate with some garden flowers. Cut them apart to make little squares. These can be mini-scrabble tiles which have the bonus feature of being thinner and lighter than the real ones. Popsicle sticks look like miniature boards. That makes them ideal to represent lumber on a page about a building or renovation projects on your home. Just snip off the rounded ends.

Children's stickers are cheaper than those from the hobby store and work great on kid-centered pages. The subjects are usually fun things that children like—animals, toys, or silly things. Sometimes they are small, but that's when you use them abundantly, like to completely frame a picture or make a page border. I found a set of fluorescent bug stickers which I have used over and over on pages about picnics, farm outings, camping trips, and garden parties.

If you just experiment with shopping in the toy aisle for scrapbooking materials, you will often find unique surprises. I found small stretched canvases imprinted with simple figures for kids to paint. I immediately bought two which I plan to join on one side with tiny hinges to make a book-like box that can be opened. The depth inside can hold a stack of folded scrapbook pages on one side and some three-dimensional mementos on the other side. It can sit on a shelf either closed as a little box or open as a stand-up frame. This would make a great mini-scrapbook gift.

I could also use a tiny piece of terrycloth to represent a miniature towel tossed against background paper featuring waves of water. A tiny rubber ducky would complete the look, or perhaps a little bar of soap made from play dough. A tiny scrapbook attached inside the right empty cavity could hold a collection of bathtub pictures featuring the grand-kids.

Or, the left side could use some dog paw-print paper as a background with glued on dog biscuits (coated with protective varnish) and my dog's old collar as an embellishment around the inside edge. The little scrapbook could hold pictures of my dog that recently died. This would look great sitting on my shelf as a token to her memory. You could do something like that for a dog-lover in your family. I'm realizing that only buying two of those little canvas frames was a big mistake.

CHAPTER 5. COMPUTER TRICKS

One of the coolest tricks I've discovered is printing black and white photos on colored copy paper. Most all photo editing programs offer the option to convert a color picture to black and white. When I made my daughter's scrapbook about her pregnancy and the birth of her daughter, I did this technique using her baby bump pose. Printed on pink paper, it looked amazing on the page which was prominently decorated with other pink items. It has become a tradition. My other daughter wanted this in her scrapbook, and then I did one in blue for my daughter-in-law who was having a boy.

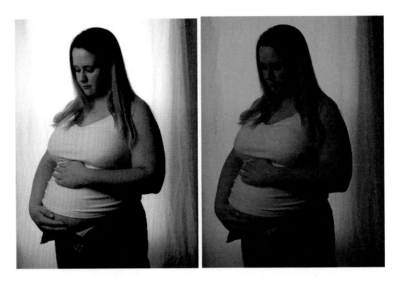

This was originally a color photo which I converted to black-and-white; then I printed it on pink paper.

With hundreds of fonts in your word processing program, there really is no need to buy letter stickers—ever. You can print your own text in every style and color imaginable. I first began to make my own titles for scrapbook pages when I needed a custom one that I couldn't find in a store. I was looking for *Diaper Party* to use on a page displaying my son-in-law's male version of a baby shower.

Most people do not even know the variety of fonts available in their programs. There are so many it's almost overwhelming, but it's really worth taking the time to look through them. Most people just use the same old ones over and over. It is a good idea, however, not to mix more than two or three on the same page. It can look a little messy and confused. And save the really fancy fonts for titles. If you are telling a story of any length, keep it simple so that it will not be too tedious to read. I love the ones that look like real cursive handwriting.

Speaking of words—why pay five dollars or more for pads of vellum quotations for your pages. I have at least four in my stockpile right now, and about ninety per cent of them I will never use. Find your own quotations online or from books, print them in whatever fancy fonts you want, and print them on vellum. Print a whole sheet full, so you don't waste that pricey paper—which is so amazing and beautiful that it is totally worth it. If you have a scrap that won't fit in your printer, try your hand at calligraphy. Or, print your text in a lovely font on plain paper exactly the way you want it on your page. Then trace over it on your scrap of vellum. Use the pointed end of a skewer to emboss your vellum words on the wrong side. No wasting expensive paper in budget scrapbooking.

There are times when vellum isn't exactly the look you're going for because you don't want the background obscured. Print your text on transparency sheets instead. This technique allows you to layer any object over, or under, another. You get a truly three-dimensional effect. Print a lovely full-color graphic along with a few descriptive words over a beautiful black-and-white portrait photo. Your page will hardly need any further embellishment.

You can actually print on cloth. This is tricky, but it looks so cool on the page. Everyone will wonder how you did it. First of all, iron the cloth completely smooth. Trim your piece to within ½ inch smaller all the way around your computer paper, then tape it to a single sheet making sure that there are no bubbles or wrinkles. Warning: if this is not done correctly, it will jam in your printer. And, do not use nappy or fuzzy materials. That might make such a mess your printer may never recover. If this technique scares you, scan a textile of your choice, then print it and use that as a background on your page. Personally, I like the real cloth better, but I tend to be daring by nature.

You can use this same technique to print on tissue paper, and it's not quite as risky. I recommend ironing it too, just to make sure it is smooth. This works well with printing photos or even clip art graphics. For a unique treatment, you can crumple the tissue after printing. Make sure the ink is very dry before doing this. I really like torn edges of tissue on these kinds of pages. To get your tears exactly where you want them cut your tissue using scissors just a little bigger than needed, then pinch off pieces along the edge between two fingers dampened with plain water.

You can find a variety of clip art in most word processing programs or those for making greeting cards. You can purchase tons of clip art CD's very cheaply. These images can be used in unique ways. I've often copied and pasted a whole line of some cute graphic to make a border. You can flip your image and use them as corners to hold down your photos. Use black and white clip art, print it out, then color it to your taste. Print multiples and layer them. Print an image in various sizes and glue them to your page in a telescoping fashion either in a straight line or in a spiral.

Change part of a graphic by combining it with another. For instance, if you find a character holding a ball, print a second image of a birthday cake, cut it out, and paste it on top of the ball to make it fit your needs. You can laminate your printed graphics to make them look shiny and give them a sturdier look. Just simple clear contact paper will make your clip art equal to any sticker you could buy in a store. Do this especially if you want to raise the image or make it three dimensional. Add glitter or other kinds of trim to make it into an embellishment to rival any you might find in a store. For a really unique treatment, print a cartoon figure and add the head of a family member from a photo.

A scanner teamed with a computer allows for lots of scrapbooking applications. I wanted to include the hand-crafted card I made on a page about a baby shower, but I wanted to save space on the page for other pictures. So, I unfolded the card, scanned it, reduced it to one quarter of the original size, then printed a little tiny card which I placed on the page in a little envelope. I used a similar technique to highlight the invitation.

Nancy and Nichole hosted a wonderful event for guests from church and family.

You can do some interesting effects just using your photos—especially funny ones. I like to cut around feet or legs on a photo and dangle them outside the frame. I like to cut out a birthday cake, or the shower cake in the previous picture, and make it pop out on the page. If your background in a picture is messy, a great solution is to cut around your subject and place it on a different background of your choice. Sometimes a tiny spring behind a picture is cute to create movement on the page. However, you will have to attach the photo after pulling the spring through your plastic page protector or you will lose the whole effect. I make my own springs by coiling wire around a pencil.

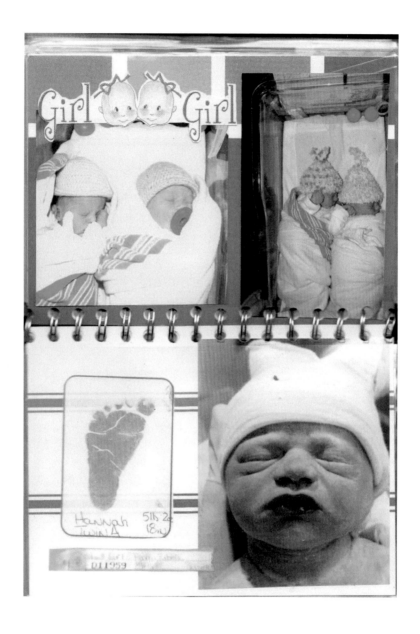

Here I scanned the footprint from the baby's I.D. card as
well as the bracelet from her foot. This not only fit better

on the page, but I could use it in both my daughter's and my own scrapbook about the new baby.

CHAPTER 6. OFFICE SUPPLIES

Simple brass brads from an office supply store cost a quarter of the price as the fancy ones in a craft store. Of course, they are plain. You can paint them with acrylic paint, and you can decorate them with glitter or put paper petals underneath them to make them into flowers. Paint them black and use them for the buttons on a snowman; not only do they give dimension—they can hold the feature to the page. Use two of them to hold a piece of string or ribbon draped across the top of the page, then dangle pennants, balloons, tags, or any shape to act as background for the lettering of a page title.

And, who says printer paper is only for printing? I accordion pleated white linen paper to make a beautiful edge for a baptism page which would work equally well for a wedding theme. I double folded some blue marble paper with a little support on the under side so that it opened in the middle like double doors to make a unique card in my baby grandson's book. Narrow blue ribbon decorated the corners and also tied the feature shut with a pretty bow.

The paper used as a border is a specialty paper from the office supply store. The background paper is a sheet of crumpled vellum.

Ordinary office tags don't look ordinary at all once you smudge the edges with ink or chalk. You can embellish them with stickers, glitter, or ribbon. Yes, the tags at the hobby store are pretty—made from vellum, foil, or special papers. But, I actually like the look of a simple utilitarian tag—and they are very sturdy, allowing you to do lots of things to them. If you need a fancy tag for some reason, use them as a template to cut your own from scraps of special paper.

I keep all my small scraps of leftover papers sorted in an accordion file folder sorted according to color. Then instead of cutting an expensive 12 x 12 sheet when all I want is a few embellishments cut from a certain color, I have it at my fingertips. In fact, often I have become so enamored of a lovely scrap of paper that I was inspired to create a whole page around it. I keep that scrap folder handy for every project.

I love the novelty notepads you find in office supply stores. These are ready-made text boxes. With all the girls in our family, I find endless ways to use the ones I found shaped like dresses and high heeled shoes. If you don't use them all, they can always work as the notepads for which they were intended. I have many varieties in stock—Christmas tree-shaped ones, Hawaiian shirt ones, and dog bone-shaped ones. You can also find regular rectangular ones that have interesting graphics or borders. And, these are very cheap.

If you are reluctant to use your own handwriting on the notepads, I see two solutions: 1) print out a smaller text box on your computer in a contrasting color, then paste it on top, or 2) print your message on blank paper, then tape your notepad sheet over the text, tape it down securely, and run it through the computer again so that it prints on top of your notepad sheet. Don't peel off the tape, just trim around it.

File folders have many uses. They make an excellent material to built structural elements in a scrapbook, and they come in colors which will not need to be covered with other paper. They take well to stickers, glitter, ink, and other embellishments, so when I use them to make pockets on a page, I seldom need to do much to disguise their appearance. File folders are actually sturdy enough to act as covers for your own home-made albums, and they are exactly the right size to hold 8 ½ x 11 pages. You don't need to cut off the tabs unless you want to; I like the look.

Use staples wherever possible to save on glue. For many heavier embellishments, a staple is better anyway. You can cover them with some other feature so they don't show, or you can actually color them before stapling with markers. Acid free glue and tape is expensive. You can avoid using these costly items and still keep your books perfectly preserved with simple staples. This is a savings that will not even show. Only you will know if six dollar tape is holding down a decoration or if it's a staple. With a little ingenuity, you can use them to hold down almost anything on your page.

It is basically the photos that are damaged by contact with acidic materials, but all the other items are held just fine with other methods. Mat your pictures with acid-free paper attaching them *after* you staple the matting down first. Right, that is quite a switch, and it takes a little extra planning to do it this way, but you will save a lot of money. Instead of attaching your matting paper to your pictures with acid free glue or tape, then attaching the matted ones to your page with more acid free glue or tape, place the mats on the page first using staples, school glue, or use brads, eyelets, or a variety of other methods. Place the pictures on after the mats. This method alone will save you about ten dollars per scrapbook, and that, in my book, is worth the extra effort at changing some habits.

Rubber cement is acid-free, it works better, and it is cheaper. I don't know how many times I have gotten exasperated over glue sticks that failed to hold my objects on the page. And, they don't go very far, either. I think they are putting less glue in those glue sticks nowadays. You can't really see how much is in there since the tubes are opaque.

The best method of using rubber cement is to apply it to both surfaces of the two objects to be joined, let it dry, then carefully place them together using a piece of wax paper between them as you move from top to bottom to assure proper placement. One of the great features I love about rubber cement is that you can un-glue the objects using rubber cement thinner. In the days before digital printing methods, all commercial art studios relied on rubber cement to do the paste-ups of their original artwork. It was an absolute staple (pun intended), and I can see why.

I also love that rubber cement is such an easy clean-up. Wait until it dries, then rub it off with your finger. That method works whether you accidentally got some excess glue on your project or whether you spilled some on your table.

When you see all the varieties of 8 ½ x 11 paper at the office supply store, you will want to make smaller albums more often. They hold fewer pictures on a page, so you will need more pages to tell your story. Make your groupings into subsets. Instead of trying to put the whole birthday party on one two-page spread, group them into scenes featuring all the different aspects of the party— eating cake, opening gifts, playing games, etc. Not only will you find 8 ½ x 11 papers in every color of the rainbow, but they are available in marble, linen, and in smaller packs of specialty papers to match every occasion from Christmas to Teacher-themed designs. I like to buy up packages of flower prints, dots, or stripes that can be used for a variety of applications. Look for off-season bargains, and try to choose themes with multiple uses. If you print a picture on linen paper, it looks like a painting on canvas and makes a beautiful portrait look very special.

But, if you really like big spreads, use the standard copy paper size in 11 x 17 fold-out sheet protectors. These are primarily used for presentation folders in the business world. Not only do they work well to display four 8 ½ x 11 pages all at once, but you can use the 11 x 17 size paper as well. It does come in several colors, it is printable in most printers, and its uses are mind boggling. You can print an expansive family tree across the entire span of four pages—using a genealogy program—then fill in with little portraits of you family members. Even without the software, you can do it yourself if you can draw straight lines and make little boxes for the names and information.

If you really want to stick with traditional 12 x 12 size you can still take advantage of the smaller sheets by joining them with tape on the back sides. If done with a design in mind, it isn't even possible to tell that it wasn't 12 x 12 paper to start with. For instance, use two colors—one in the middle and another on the two ends. Use a page border at the bottom or at the top to fill the one inch gap. Or, use three or more colors, trimming your sheets in half lengthwise by laying them horizontally. You will have an inch to spare along the side of the page, but use a page border for that. There are many ways to accommodate smaller paper onto big pages. (See Illustration.)

two ways to join 8 1/2 x 11 paper
to make 12 x 12 pages

Even the borders are ordinary copy paper cut with decorative scissors.

Don't overlook the humble label maker. They have greatly improved since their early days. It makes very cute title and text applications on a scrapbook page. The tape comes in a variety of colors, and many label makers offer a few different fonts and sizes for lettering. The letters are raised, making for several different ways to use them. If you are going for the "distressed" look, paint your strips of words before peeling off the protective film on the back, then use a light sandpaper—an emery board works well for this—and scratch off the paint on just the raised letters. This makes a cool sort of grunge effect.

CHAPTER 7. HARDWARE STORES

I have a secret passion for hardware stores. It was only natural that I would find some scrapbooking applications while enjoying the sights and smells as I perused the aisles.

If you think about it, the construction of a room is not that much different than creating a scrapbook page—designing, cutting, and piecing it all together. The tools and materials are just bigger.

Metal washers are great for a masculine page or for a teenage heavy metal treatment. Use great big ones as frames for circular pictures. Use smaller ones in a row for a page edge. Use them to hold individual letters to make a really bold title. Glue sequins or jewels inside the hole to make a spectacular eye-catcher. Washers are nice because they lie flat, they glue easily, and you can write on them with a sharpie.

I found a manufacturer online who make over 26,000 varieties of washers. You can search for them on their website according to inside diameter, outside diameter, and thickness. They offer washers made of aluminum, brass, copper, nickel, stainless steel, and titanium. Their illustrations showed washers in colors like red, green, yellow, and orange, but I have no idea what they were made of—probably polyester or nylon. They also make custom orders from clients. You would need to buy at least 100 items to place an order with this company, but this just gives you an idea of what is out there. Ask if your local hardware store can get you the size and colors you need.

Twine and wire here are typically half the price than at the hobby shops. I found a spool for ninety-seven cents that is one-third the price of a similar amount sold for crafting. You just need to remember to stick with small gauges, and you can find poly-wrapped wiring in the electrical department. It comes in lots of color choices. These are perfect for twisting into shapes or letters. Green or red make perfect Christmas shapes. Make a green tree shape, then cover it with green netting, and you can decorate it with little charm ornaments. And, what is the perfect way to attach your wire letters and shapes? More wire, of course. Use fine wire cut into tiny lengths to pierce through your paper like a staple. Twist it open on the back side, cover it with a piece of tape, and you have a secure and attractive attachment. I used this method to attach wire **e**'s when I ran out of the sticker letters I was using. It looked very deliberate, and I liked it so much I decided to use this method on other pages.

This is a great way to use up leftover letters when the ones you need are missing. I placed pictures on tags covered with decorative paper and put them in a pocket. The leaf pattern was cut from a cookie cutter, the tiger from a brochure, and the butterflies are kid stickers.

A little bit of metal or vinyl screening material can be a perfect effect on a summer page. Make a little screen door that opens to expose a partially hidden photo or embellishment. Of course, you probably don't want to buy a whole roll of this material. If you can't find any leftovers in your garage or workshop, buy a screen repair kit. It includes several small patches of screen cloth as well as the fine wire needed to sew up your repair.

Chicken wire, if it's fine enough, has an amazing geometric pattern that I love. Unless you have a barnyard out back, it might not be so easy to come by, however. I have found some furnace filters which have a similar-looking wire structure inside the layers. *Caution: Be sure to use gloves and a mask when tearing them apart. Some contain fiberglass.*

Sheet metal grill work comes in really attractive designs. It is barely thin enough to work on a scrapbook page, but you need metal snips to cut it. Be careful and wear protective gloves. You can buy small pieces of this material, and though thin, it actually is sturdy enough to use for scrapbook covers. Bend it into shape using a straight board. Attach rings right through the grill pattern to hold your pages inside. Or, drill holes for the rings and attach them with metal bolts and washers.

Tiny hinges and clasps made of metal are really cool to make things that actually open and close on your page. This can take the form of any object—a pirate's chest, a jewelry box, or a tiny window pane. I have used flat corner braces as borders. Instead of screws, fill the empty holes with play dough, press a slit down the center so that it looks like a screw, and paint it silver to finish it off.

Metallic lettering for attaching a street address or mark your mailbox make shiny spectacular page titles. They come in smaller sizes, too, and they are designed to be seen easily. Thus you will have an eye-catching title in silver or gold tones.

Use sandpaper both as a tool and as a decorative element on a page. Sand off layers of color for a rustic look. Sand the edges of photographs for an artistic effect. Cut your scissors through sandpaper five or six times to sharpen them. This works for your punches, too. And, a sandpaper mat behind a photo makes for a nice masculine looking page. Of course glue won't stick to sandpaper, so you need to use wire, brads, or clips to attach the picture. Using wood letters on sandpaper makes a great page title. Drill tiny little holes through the letters and the brads will look like nails—or screws if you draw a line through the middle. Cut out shapes or letters from sandpaper, too. Slice it into strips to make stripes or borders on your page.

Sawdust is not something you can actually buy in your home improvement store. But it is easy to make, or you can just sweep it off the floor of someone's workshop. Use sawdust by sprinkling it in glue just like you would glitter. Run a piece of double-sided tape through a pile of sawdust then attach it to your page as an edging. Be careful not to get any sawdust on the wrong side of your tape or it will not stick, and it will have bumps in it. Instead of double-sided tape, use a roll of window insulating tape. This is the tape used to attach plastic sheeting to window frames. The adhesive on this material is super strong.

Wallpaper samples may not be acid-free, but they make great background papers. Sometimes the surface is treated with some substance that repels glue, but you can attach your scrapbook features using brads, wire, ribbon, or staples. The manufacturers are thinking more of families who want to wipe off stains more so than scrapbookers who are drawn to their designs.

The background is a wallpaper sample. The pages are attached with eyelets and strung together with ribbon.

Paint chips have become so popular for crafting that stores have a difficult time keeping them in stock. Part of their appeal is that they are free. I like the ones that show gradations of the same color. You can punch shapes out of these colorful strips or use them to write text on. They can become almost any element on a page.

Decals sold in hardware stores are meant to be used on walls or on furniture. But, they will work on paper, too. The dry application kind is preferable, since you don't want to get your scrapbook wet. If you find a design you really like, there is probably a way to work around the application methods. You might apply them to another sheet of paper first, let it dry, then trim around the edges before placing it on your page.

Chain is attractive on a page—as long as it is thin enough. I have used the beaded style chain used for light pulls to frame a picture, for instance. The obvious uses come to mind when thinking about more masculine pages, but chain can be pretty, too. Use the very fine open weave type used for toy box lids by weaving ribbon or yarn between the spaces. Dangle charms or jewels from it.

Use Spackle and a plastic stencil for dimensional effects on a page. Tape a snowflake stencil to your page then smear the Spackle into the openings, smoothing it flat with a spatula. Lift the stencil when it becomes almost completely firm. Let it dry until completely hard before attempting to work with it further. You can paint your design or add glitter.

Plywood is not thin enough to cut into shapes and letters for your pages, but it is easy enough to construct into an album. I saw a wooden scrapbook which was selling for over thirty dollars. Wood is beautiful just raw, but it is possible to finish it with stain or varnish or even paint it with colors. You could do a fancy wood burning effect on the cover. Or, you could use those decals you found on the other aisle. If you can use basic tools and can cut straight edges, you can make a custom scrapbook yourself—or perhaps with the help of a friend who does woodworking. There are several possible ways to attach hinges, rings, or posts to hold your pages. You could use simple bolts with nuts and washers to act as posts. (See Illustration.)

Bolts are used as posts to hold together the pages; tiny hinges allow you to open the book. The back cover is just a solid piece of wood. I stenciled on the words using dark stain.

Foam weather-stripping tape works just as well as a similar product sold in craft stores. You just snip off sections and apply it to the back of various decorative elements to raise them off the page. The only advantage to the expensive stuff is that is adhesive backed on both sides. For the savings involved, I am willing to apply a dab of glue to the plain side.   The weather-stripping is actually quite a bit thicker than the craft store version, and I actually like the added height.

I love shopping in hardware stores anyway, and if you haven't tried it, you should. Go up and down every aisle because you never know when you are going to find some unusual item that you can adapt to scrapbooking.

CHAPTER 8. RESALE SHOPS

Gently used scrapbooking materials can often be found in the hobby section at resale shops. It's hard to believe that people would actually donate materials we go out and spend money for. You know what they say about one man's trash being another man's treasure! Sometimes there is a need to weed out our duplicate or overflowing stash—to make room for more. I have found real bargains in the resale shops, including a six-inch thick stack of beautifully patterned and flocked papers. I got the whole bundle for five dollars, and grabbed up over fifty sheets of top quality papers.

I never pass by the book section because old pages and sheet music are great finds. Cut them, fold them, or print a graphic or photo right over the words.   You can re-purpose old books and make unique keepsakes. Since you wouldn't want to make a 200-page scrapbook, tear out every third page or so.   Then glue every two pages together to add thickness and sturdiness to your pages.   I suggest rubber cement for this and a two-inch brush to cut down on this time-consuming task. Ink directly over the printed pages with stamping or cover them with scraps of paper, cloth, or other materials. Glue on photos, feathers, charms, textiles, and whatever suits your inclination to make a re-born book that could be a special gift for someone.

This scrapbook cover was made with a folded place-mat. I folded it off-center so that 8 ½ x 11 paper would fit and so that the page edging would show. The Santa picture is a torn page from an old children's book.

I once found a brocade dress in a re-sale shop that I wouldn't have been caught dead wearing. Apparently neither did the owner. But, cut to size, pressed with a hot iron, and voila—it became the new cover for a worn scrapbook with ugly damages which I had found on another shopping trip. Two lessons in one here: 1) Shop the clothing aisles looking for pretty cloth, buttons, etc., and 2) Don't overlook an album with good structure just because of a few surface flaws. Sometimes all it will take is a strategically placed adornment to fix it up, or take it completely apart and re-cover it for a beautiful brand new look.

Search for spools of ribbon, packages of yarn, stencils, holiday trimmings, and leftover party goods. You will find grab bags of buttons, lace, and sewing notions that might not be enough for an outfit but would be just right on your page. Artificial flowers used are a tenth of the cost new ones. Don't worry that they're too thick for a scrapbook. Tear apart the petals, pull off the leaves, or use them on the outside of your scrapbook. Sometimes a nice stiff place-mat from the housewares section can work as a scrapbook cover. Just fold it in half, punch holes in the middle, and insert your pages tying them in with a cord. Use small doilies by spraying them with glue then sticking them to your background paper. I once found a huge bag of feathers, and it tickled the heck out of me all the way home.

Old magazines have many uses, too. Roll the pages tightly and use like pipe cleaners to make lettering. Cut them into strips and weave them for a colorful backdrop. Tear out scenic pages to use as background paper. Ads are geared to be eye-catching, and so will those interesting graphics spruce up your pages. Even if you are a pretty good photographer yourself, face it—you are not likely to have access to spectacular pictures of the foreign places and exotic creatures—not unless you steal them from magazines like National Geographic. It is okay to steal these images, as long as you don't *sell* your scrapbooks.

If you do this for your own personal use or as a gift for friends or family, there is no need to worry about copyright infringement. Keep this example in mind. A friend made a tee shirt for me expressing my tender feelings for Elvis. I wore it on a trip to Graceland and was promptly stopped by someone who looked very authoritative. He wanted to know where I bought the shirt. When I explained, he let me off the hook. Whew! Elvis Presley Enterprises, Inc. is extremely possessive about their copyrights. This is why I did not include or recommend any purchased graphics, stickers, or embellishments of any kind in this book. I would have needed to get permission to use them. This may or may not have involved a charge. But, the real problem is that after I use something on a page and throw away the packaging, I can no longer remember the name of the manufacturer. Anyway, the whole idea here is that you make your own features and use your own creativity.

CHAPTER 9. NATURE—ALMOST

Real flowers, foliage, seed pods, and leaves might look lovely adorning a page, but they carry with them tiny microbes, mold, and insects that we do not want in our house, much less in our precious works of art. Fake ones are an option, and the expensive ones are difficult to distinguish from the real thing. That would defy the purpose of budget scrapbooking, however. But, there are ways to achieve the same look and not spend a lot of money.

Pressed flowers are so easy to make, but they take time. That is why ones you buy in a store are so costly. Someone has to collect the blooms, press them between absorbent papers with heavy weights, and then preserve them. You can do all of that using an old book or a few pieces of wood.

Layer the flowers between the covers of a book or between two boards clamped together tightly in the following order: top wood (or book cover), cardboard, blotting paper (like newspaper), white paper, flowers, white paper, blotting paper, cardboard, bottom wood. Allow them to dry for about two weeks, changing the blotting paper every two or three days. Leaves can be pressed just like flowers. To assure that microscopic life is not hiding inside your embellishments, seal your pieces with a light coat of clear silicone sealer.

You can make nature prints with leaves and flowers from outside, too. Coat a beautiful specimen of your choice with a layer of strong blue on the smooth side of the leaf. Attach it to a block of wood to use as your handle. The veins and stems can now be used as a rubber stamp in paint or ink of your choice.

The reverse process also creates a beautiful effect. Choose a piece of art paper to use as your scrapbook page. Arrange your foliage on it, then spray paint in a color that will become your background. Remove the plants and the unpainted area will reveal the silhouette of your flowers. Since the plants are not glued to the paper, your imprint will have a very artsy look.

There is an age old tradition of collecting a clump of hair and tying it with a ribbon for a sweet remembrance about baby's first haircut. It actually can work to record teenagers' many changes in hair color along with pictures showing their differing styles through the years. These mementos become more meaningful as time passes, and memories needn't be limited only to infancy. Children may only remember their grandparents as having gray hair. This would be a nice way to show them the original color. If kept in an envelope on the page, future generations can take it out and compare the color to their own.

Feathers are natural works of art and also look great on scrapbook pages. Just make sure they are clean, if you are getting them from the barnyard or the woods. Guard against any possibility of contamination if you are collecting feathers from sources of which you are in any way unsure. Although rare, infections can be deadly serious. Use rubber gloves to pick them up, boil them, and then dry them on paper towels. If you want to take the effort, a hair dryer makes them fluffier, and you will be able to use them sooner. You might want to snatch a few from the bottom of your pet bird's cage to show his true colors next to his picture.

EMILY

Emily will always
have a place in my
heart because she
wanted to be a mother
so badly that she
adopted Ruby's baby
ducks.

This is a page from my scrapbook about my farm animals. I cut out a section from the foreground and blew it up to become the background paper because I did not want actual straw in my book. The feather is hers, however.

Sand from the beach where you vacationed can be used in any way you would use glitter. Besides being pretty, it will be very meaningful in years to come. Coat the lettering for your page title with adhesive then dip them into your sand before placing them on the page. You could also put a teaspoon of sand into a bubble window made from cellophane. Seal the edges liberally with acrylic compound. Be sure to label the sand as to where it is from so that future generations will be able to enjoy it, too. It may not look any different from what you could get at a construction site, so you need to let everyone know how special it is.

Rubbings done with craft paper and wax crayons or chalk are most commonly done on gravestones. But, they can be done on smaller items as well—so that they can fit into a scrapbook. Why not make a rubbing of the license plate on a first car? A favorite pet's tags or collar? Military I.D. tags that belong to a beloved service man or woman? A very special engraved piece of jewelry?

CHAPTER 10. INTERNET SOURCES

Online, you can get free downloads of patterns, ideas, fonts, stencils, etc. Best would be to go to trusted websites, and see what they have to offer. Lots of legitimate good deals are out there.

Pinterest is a great place where much information is shared without cost. Browse the *DIY and Crafts* category, not only *scrapbooking*. I have found many tips for other crafts that could be applied to scrapbooking. You can trust Kim Komando's freebies, too. Facebook has a lot of links to crafting pages. Watch out though, some of them are selling stuff that is pretty irresistible.

Go to the website for your printer manufacturer. They tend to offer lots of free stuff to download and lots of ideas for craft projects. And, you don't need to stick to your own brand. Try all the printer websites for down-loadable graphics and idea pages.

Right-clicking allows you to pull logos and pictures from restaurants, stores, hotels, or other places for use on your pages if they represent the places in your pictures. It is perfectly legal to do this for your own personal use. You just can't put them in books you intend to sell. I did this once to get some really good pictures of a hotel where we stayed. We were so busy taking fun family shots that when we arrived home and I realized that I didn't have any photos that showed off some of the great features we wanted to remember. Most of the chains are proud to display their amenities, comfortable rooms, and scenic settings.

Family Fun

STONEY CREEK INN & CONFERENCE CENTER

We had a fun "staycation" an hour from home.

You can find great deals on scrapbooking supplies and tools on eBay, Craigslist, etc. Sometimes you will find whole collections when someone is giving up the hobby. Every once in a while, someone does weeding of their stash and offers economical bundles of supplies. That is not a bad idea to make room in your own collection. You will occasionally find some unique embellishment for sale that is either a vintage piece or something hand-crafted.

Search for coupons and sales at all the craft store sites. Just about any store you can think of sells online nowadays. Many offer copies of their mailers on their website, and sometimes you will find "online only" deals and "print your own" coupons.

FINAL WORDS

A new phenomenon has invaded the world of scrapbooking—printed books made from online applications that permit you to make digital scrapbooks at their sites. I'm not saying there aren't some advantages to this method—the main being that other family members can purchase multiple copies of the same book, ending sibling rivalry. But, I still hold that these are not *real* scrapbooks. They are photo books. I like to see texture on a page; I like cutting, piecing, and crafting one-of-a-kind books. To me, the fact that there is only one makes it all the more special. Or, maybe I just like the smell of glue.

These photo books can be quite beautiful, and the price has come down considerably since they first began. These sites allow you to store unlimited amounts of uploaded pictures forever on their sites. That alone is a great feature and a good reason for giving this a try. They often have amazing offers and sales throughout the year, so I can't say it isn't a bargain. Most of them allow you to work in much the same way as regular scrapbooking—choosing backgrounds, layouts, embellishments, and adding your own text. This doesn't have to be and "either or" situation. You can enjoy both methods.

Before closing this book, I want to share one final idea for re-claiming some of your unused photos and making them into something really special. I just couldn't toss some of the "mistake" photos of our family members—ones where someone had a funny expression, was caught bending over, or an accidentally snapped a frame showing a crazy angle or compromising view where one body part appeared disproportionate. I made an entire scrapbook of all I could find which I titled *My Funny Family*, and I used it as an exchange gift at our family Christmas gathering. They literally fought over who would go home with that book. I felt so sorry for the loser that had re-prints made and re-created the whole thing just for her. I plan to make another one for myself and other members of the family. This is where my digital scrapbooking daughter argues that it could have been available for everyone had I done it online. I'm thinking I just might do that after all. I never would have thought that this simple book made from "junk" photos would ever have become such a hit. I think everyone should try this.

I'm not saying you can't occasionally spend an elaborate amount of money on a very special scrapbook. Saving money most of the time can allow you to splurge once in a while. Shop the expensive hobby stores, but try to think how you can make it yourself or get it somewhere else cheaper. And throughout all your regular shopping chores in all the bargain bins, the off-season aisles, and the discount stores—shop always with scrapbooking in mind.

I hope you enjoyed and found all these scrapbooking ideas useful. To your success!

Made in the USA
Lexington, KY
10 March 2018